Contents

About the Author 1

Introduction 1

Veggie Patterns

Artichokes 2
Carrots 5
Cauliflower 8
Corn 11
Eggplant 14
Kohlrabi 17
Peas 20
Peppers 23
Squash 26
Tomatoes 29

About the Author

Combining sewing and drawing is a natural for Bea Oglesby. She considers gardens, flowers, and nature endless sources of ideas for appliqué. Although Bea did not start quilting until the mid-1980s, she has sewn most of her life having three daughters and a background in home economics. Bea has lived in Japan and has a certificate in Japanese flower arranging. She has also studied art, including charcoal sketching, oils, and watercolors.

Bea teaches and lectures in her community and belongs to several quilt guilds. She is also a volunteer in the community and at the Johnson County Library. She lives in Kansas with her husband. Other American Quilter's Society books by Bea include *Butterfly Album* (2004), *Birds and Flowers Album* (2003), and *Wildflower Album: Appliqué & Embroidery Patterns* (2000).

Introduction

The 10 vegetable patterns can be used as a single design or can be combined to use as a quilt.

The amount of fabric needed for your project will depend on what you plan to make. Feel free to change my color selections to blend with your background fabric of choice.

©2013, from *Veggies from the Good Earth Appliqué Album* (AQS, 2006)

Veggie Patterns

Artichokes

ar·ti·choke 1 : a tall Mediterranean composite herb *(Cynara scolymus)* resembling a thistle with coarse pinnately incised leaves; also : its edible immature flower head which is cooked as a vegetable

77 Pieces

Veggie Patterns - Artichokes

Do not let the number of pieces scare you. This is not a difficult pattern to appliqué.

Color

Only two fabrics were used in this pattern. One was a mottled green for the stalks and leaves. The petals of the globe artichoke were appliquéd with one green-and-violet batik fabric. By fussy cutting the individual pieces, it was not difficult to distinguish between the petals, having the pink and violet shades at the top and the green shades near the stems. When appliquéing the artichokes, work with one at a time and complete it before you start the next one. In this way, you are able to critique your color choices.

Appliqué Tips

Leave a small section of stalk 3 open where leaf 53 attaches. After leaf 53 is appliquéd, sew down this section of stalk 3.

Finishing

The veins on the leaves can be quilted during the final quilting of the pattern.

4 • The Quilter's Veggie Garden • Bea Oglesby

Carrots

car·rot 1 : a biennial herb (*Daucus carota* of the family *Umbelliferae*, the carrot family) with a usually orange spindle-shaped edible root; also : its root

19 Pieces

Cauliflower

cau·li·flow·er : a garden plant *(Brassica oleracea botrytis)* related to the cabbage and grown for its compact edible head of usually white undeveloped flowers; also : its flower cluster used as a vegetable

23 Pieces

Carrots

car·rot 1 : a biennial herb (*Daucus carota* of the family *Umbelliferae*, the carrot family) with a usually orange spindle-shaped edible root; also : its root

19 Pieces

Veggie Patterns - Carrots

For needle-turn appliqué, add a ¼" turn-under allowance, then trim closer when appliquéing.

Veggie Patterns - Carrots

Color

This pattern consists of three different medium shades of green fabric for the leaf stems and two different shades of orange for the carrots.

Finishing

To achieve the lacy look of carrot leaves, embroider the leaves with three strands of floss and a stem stitch. Start the embroidery right at the tips of the stems and match the floss to the color of the stem fabric.

For needle-turn appliqué, add a ¼" turn-under allowance, then trim closer when appliquéing.

Cauliflower

cau·li·flow·er : a garden plant *(Brassica oleracea botrytis)* related to the cabbage and grown for its compact edible head of usually white undeveloped flowers; also : its flower cluster used as a vegetable

23 Pieces

Veggie Patterns - Cauliflower

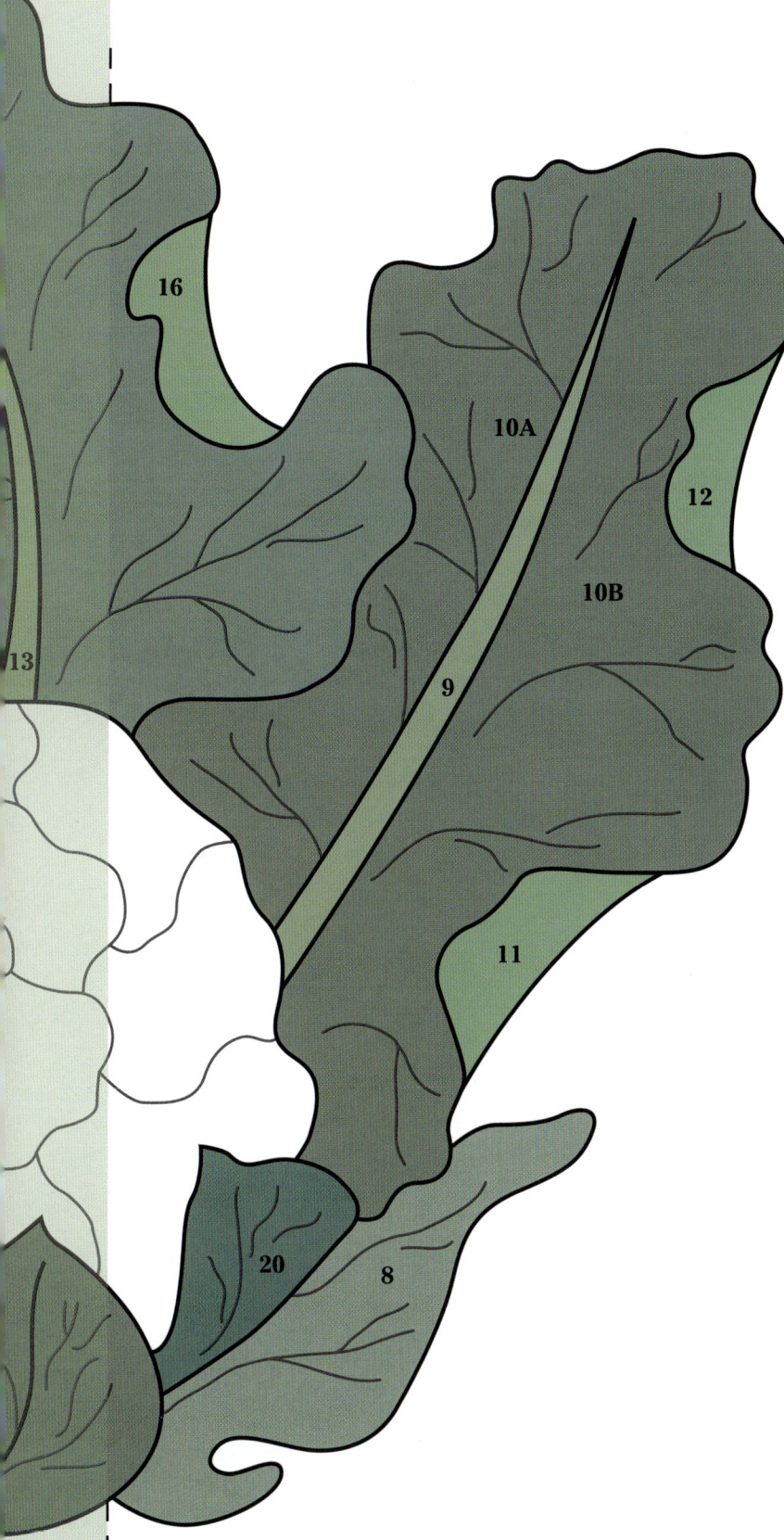

Color

One white fabric was used for the cauliflower. If the background shadows through the white fabric, it is wise to line the cauliflower, which will give you a much sharper image. To line, cut a piece of white muslin the exact size of the cauliflower pattern and baste it onto the background fabric. Appliqué the cauliflower fabric over the lining. A light green was used for the veins in the leaves and the leaf turnover. Several shades of deeper green were used for the leaves.

Appliqué Tips

To get a very narrow vein in the leaves, appliqué the lower section of the leaf stem in place with the seam allowance turned under. Baste the vein fabric that is under the leaf onto the background. Cut the leaf patterns 6, 10, 14 and 23 in half on the vein line and label them A and B. Treat these leaves as two pieces. Appliqué A first, then B. In this way, a narrow vein can be achieved. On the tips of the leaves, whip part B over part A with tiny stitches.

Finishing

Small veins in the leaves and cauliflower florets can be quilted during the final quilting of the pattern.

For needle-turn appliqué, add a ¼" turn-under allowance, then trim closer when appliquéing.

Veggie Patterns – Cauliflower

Corn

corn : 1 : a small hard seed 2 a : the seeds of a cereal grass and especially of the important cereal crop of a particular region (as wheat in Britain, oats in Scotland and Ireland, and Indian corn in the New World and Australia) b : the kernels of sweet corn served as a vegetable while still soft and milky

25 Pieces

Veggie Patterns - Corn

For needle-turn appliqué, add a ¼" turn-under allowance, then trim closer when appliquéing.

For needle-turn appliqué, add a ¼" turn-under allowance, then trim closer when appliquéing.

Color

Four different green fabrics were used for the corn husks, two shades of brown for 24 and 25, and six different shades of gold for the corn.

Appliqué Tips

For each ear of corn, cut two strips of fabric ¾" x 12" of six gold fabrics. Sew these 12 strips together, alternating the fabrics with a scant ¼" seam allowance. Press flat with all the seam allowances open for less bulk on the back of the pieced strips. From the pieced strips, cut ¾" wide strips perpendicular to the seams. Sew these strips back together, offsetting colors to create the look of corn kernels. You do not have to be accurate in sewing these strips together. Corn kernels are different sizes. Press seam allowances open and flat with a steam iron. Place pattern pieces 1 and 17 on your newly-made fabric, mark, cut out with a seam allowance, and appliqué.

Finishing

For the corn silk, embroider with two strands of yellow or gold floss using the stem stitch.

Eggplant

egg·plant : 1 a : a widely cultivated perennial Asian herb *(Solanum melongena)* of the nightshade family yielding edible fruit b : the usually smooth ovoid typically blackish-purple or white fruit of the eggplant

27 Pieces

Veggie Patterns - Eggplant

Color

Hand-dyed lavender was used for the flowers – two or three shades of lavender would work as well. There are many shades of eggplant. Use any color you desire, but choose two different fabrics to distinguish one eggplant from another. Use three different green fabrics in the leaves for variety.

Appliqué Tips

Leave a small section of 17 open until 22 is appliquéd, then complete 17. Leave a small section of 22 open until 27 is appliquéd, then complete 22.

Finishing

Embroider the stamens in the flowers with black floss. The veins can be quilted during the final quilting of the pattern.

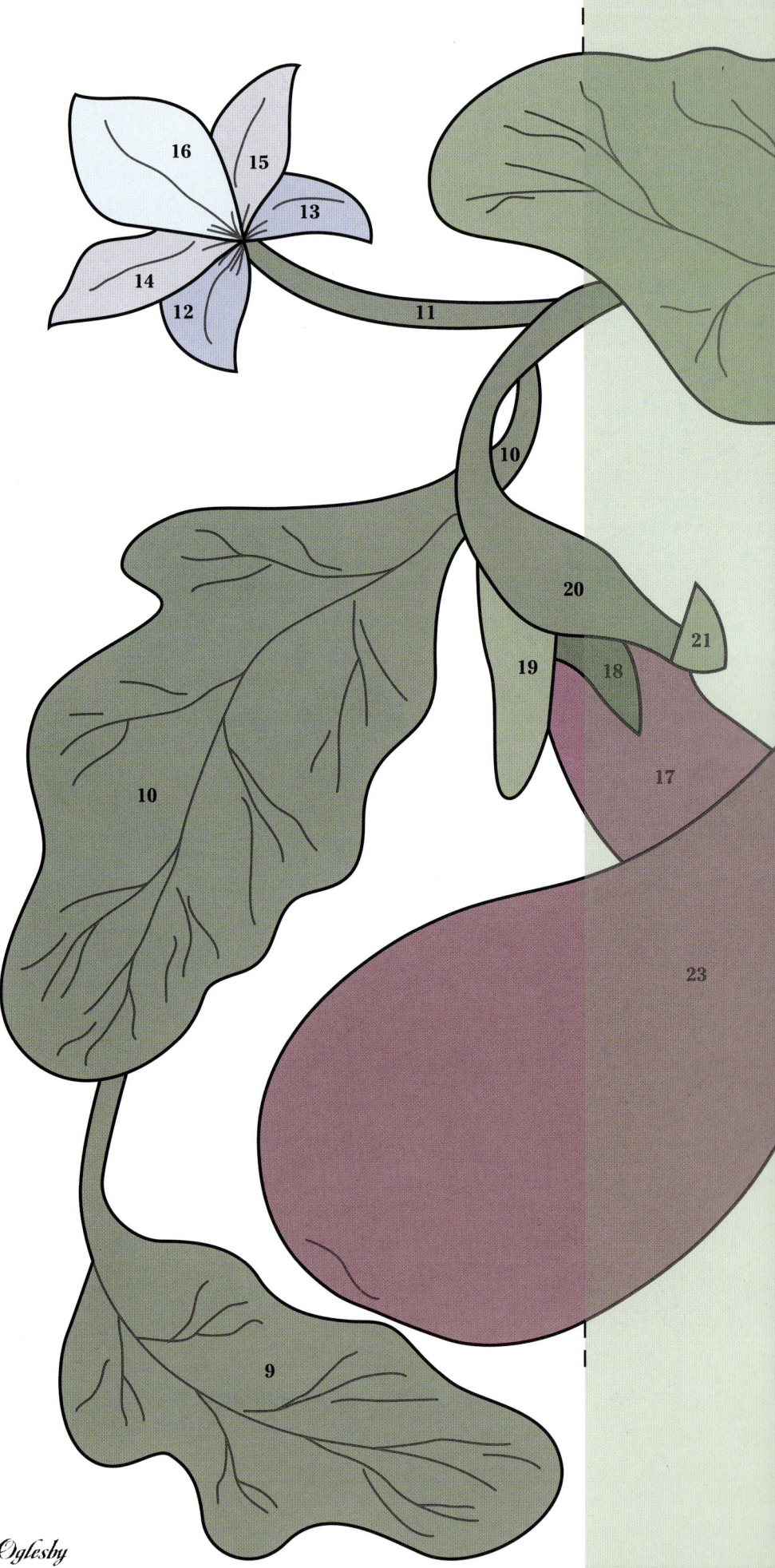

Veggie Patterns - Kohlrabi

Color
For the kohlrabi, use a very pale green, off-white, or greenish yellow fabric. Use a deeper shade of the kohlrabi fabric for the stems. Use two or three shades of deep green for the leaves so that each leaf will be distinct.

Appliqué Tips
For a very narrow vein in the leaves, appliqué and baste the vein fabric onto the background in the same manner as the cauliflower (page 9).

Finishing
The veins in the leaves can be quilted during the final quilting of the pattern.

For needle-turn appliqué, add a ¼" turn-under allowance, then trim closer when appliquéing.

Veggie Patterns - Kohlrabi

Bea Oglesby • The Quilter's Veggie Garden   19

Peas

pea 1 a : a variable annual Eurasian vine *(Pisum sativum)* of the legume family that is cultivated especially for its rounded smooth or wrinkled edible protein-rich seeds b : the seed of the pea c plural : the immature pods of the pea with their included seeds

38 Pieces

Veggie Patterns - Peas

Color
Three different green fabrics were used for the peas, pods, stems, and leaves. The peas should be light against the dark pod and the stems should be dark to contrast against leaf 1. Use two shades of pink for the buds.

Appliqué Tips
Make all the peas the same size. To make peas, cut a circle from an index card the size of the pea pattern. Cut out a fabric circle adding a ¼" seam allowance and run a basting stitch around the circle. Place the cardboard circle on the wrong side of the fabric and draw up the basting thread to gather. When the fabric is tight around the circle, press to keep the fabric in place. Remove the cardboard and place the peas on pod pieces 29 and 30. Slip stitch in place. Cover a portion of the peas with the remaining pods, 31 and 32.

Finishing
Embroider the pea vine with two strands of floss using a stem stitch.

For needle-turn appliqué, add a ¼" turn-under allowance, then trim closer when appliquéing.

Bea Oglesby • The Quilter's Veggie Garden

Veggie Patterns - Peas

For needle-turn appliqué, add a ¼" turn-under allowance, then trim closer when appliquéing.

Peppers

pep·per : CAPSICUM 1a; especially : a New World capsicum *(Capsicum annuum)* whose fruits are hot peppers or sweet peppers b : the hollow fruit of a pepper that is usually red or yellow when ripe

19 Pieces

Veggie Patterns – Peppers

Color
Three shades of green were used for the leaves and stems. A darker green was used for the inside of leaf 4. The buds are white. If your background is white, yellow or off-white fabric can be used. If your background shadows through, the buds may need to be lined. Use the same method as the cauliflower (page 9). You have many choices for your peppers – red, green, yellow, orange, or different shades of each. Be sure that pieces 1 and 17 are a deeper shade of the pepper color used.

Finishing
The veins in the leaves and peppers can be quilted during the final quilting of the pattern.

For needle-turn appliqué, add a ¼" turn-under allowance, then trim closer when appliquéing.

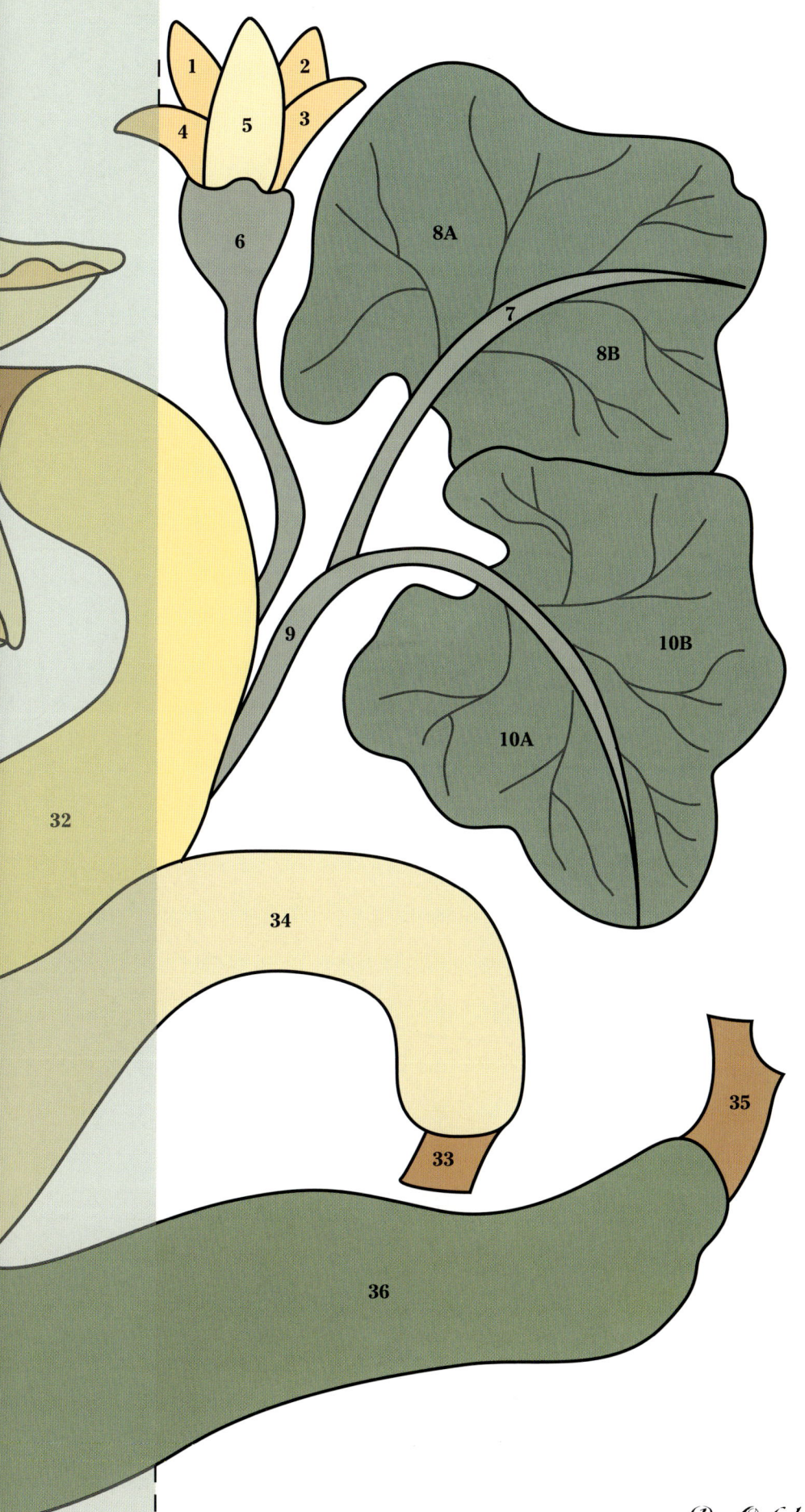

Veggie Patterns – Squash

Color
Two shades of light and dark gold were used for the bud and flower. The squash can be gold, green, or yellow. Two light and dark green fabrics were used for the leaves.

Appliqué Tips
Appliqué the leaves and the leaf veins in the same manner as the cauliflower (page 9). For the squash flower, baste 15, 18, 21, 24, and 27 in place on the background and appliqué the flower edges over this dark center using a lighter shade of gold.

Finishing
The smaller veins in the leaves can be quilted during the final quilting of the pattern.

For needle-turn appliqué, add a ¼" turn-under allowance, then trim closer when appliquéing.

Bea Oglesby • The Quilter's Veggie Garden — 27

Veggie Patterns - Squash

For needle-turn appliqué, add a ¼" turn-under allowance, then trim closer when appliquéing.

Tomatoes

to·ma·to : 1 : the usually large rounded typically red or yellow pulpy berry of an herb (genus *Lycopersicon*) of the nightshade family native to South America 2 : a plant that produces tomatoes; especially : one *(Lycopersicon esculentum* syn. *L. lycopersicum)* that is a tender perennial widely cultivated as an annual for its edible fruit

22 Pieces

Veggie Patterns - Tomatoes

Color
Three different red fabrics were used for the tomatoes. One green fabric was used for the leaves and another green for the stems.

Appliqué Tips
On piece 13, leave one of the stems loose until stem 22 is appliquéd. Leave the tip of leaf 21 loose until stem 22 is in place. After 22 is appliquéd, sew the loose parts of 13 and 21.

Finishing
Leaf veins can be quilted during the final quilting of the pattern.

For needle-turn appliqué, add a ¼" turn-under allowance, then trim closer when appliquéing.

More AQS Books

This is only a small selection of the books available from the American Quilter's Society. AQS books are known worldwide for timely topics, clear writing, beautiful color photos, and accurate illustrations and patterns. The following books are available from your local bookseller, quilt shop, or public library.

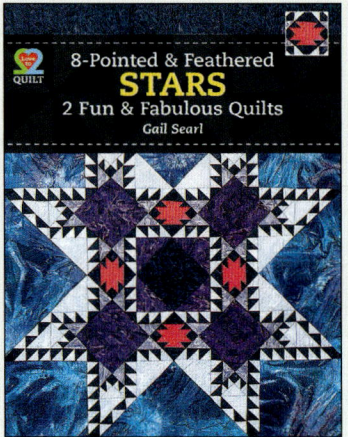
#1284

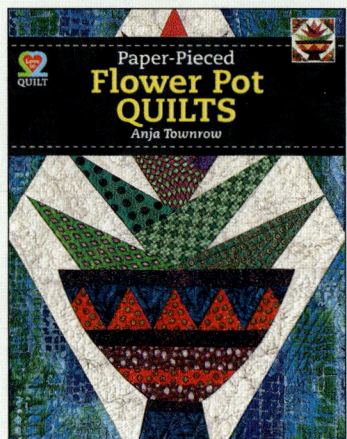
#1288

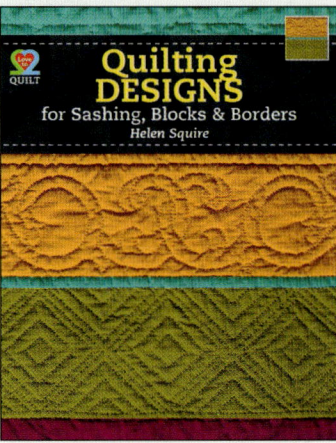
#1286

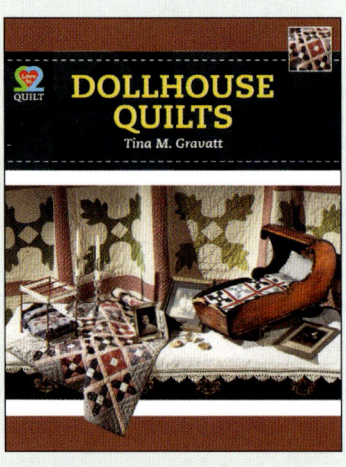
#1290

#1292

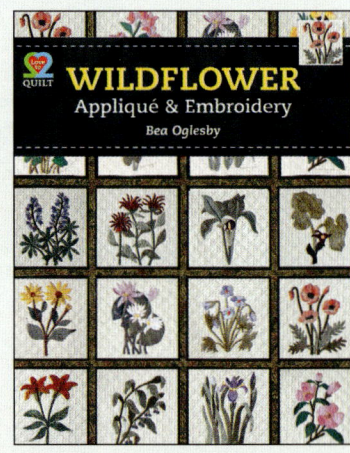
#1289

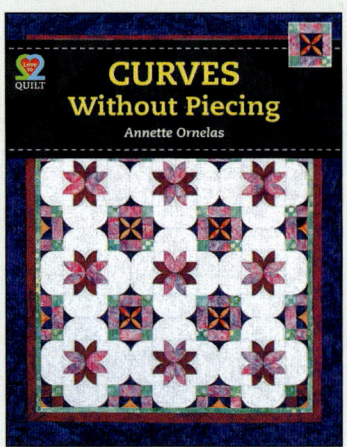
#1293

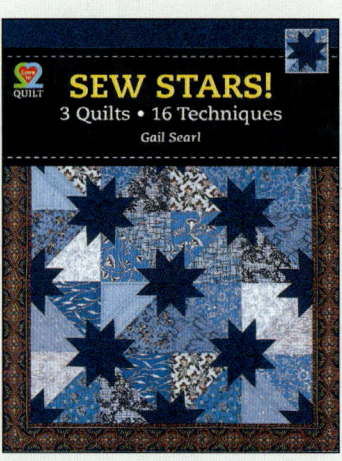
#1295

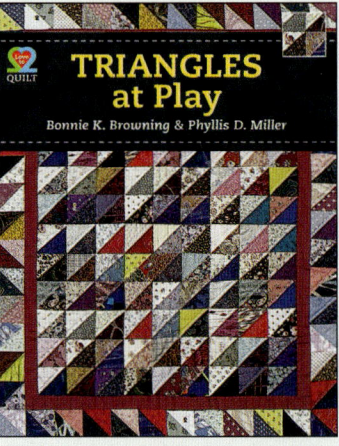
#1297

LOOK for these books nationally.
CALL or **VISIT** our website at

1-800-626-5420
www.AmericanQuilter.com